What You S[...] Know About...

PETS

Table of Contents

A Tale of Two Tails...and a Fight! 2

One Life, Not Nine 6

Breathing Underwater...........................8

Lovebirds in Love? 10

Training a Hamster............................12

Cat and Mouse 14

Homeward Bound..............................16

Fish Without Eggs.............................18

Night Vision? 20

Talking with Dogs 22

"Parroting" Language 24

In Living Color 26

Homing Instinct 28

Your Turn 30

Glossary.....................................31

Index..32

by Nancy White

A Tale of Two Tails...and a Fight!

A big, fluffy, white dog named Harold was trotting along with his owner on a trail just north of New York City in the United States. Midnight, a large, black dog with floppy ears, was approaching with his owner from the opposite direction. Both dogs' tails were straight up and wagging rapidly, so their owners decided to let the dogs play. Big mistake! In an instant, the dogs were growling, snarling, and snapping. A major fight was in progress. Fortunately, both dogs were on leashes, so the owners were able to pull the dogs apart before they could hurt each other.

The humans were shocked at their dogs' behavior. The problem was that they were both first-time dog owners, and they hadn't done their research. They believed, as most people do, that a wagging tail means a happy, friendly dog. They didn't know that different wags can have different meanings.

This dog might be saying, "Let's play."

Animal **behaviorists**—scientists who study animal behaviors and their meanings—have learned by observation that a slow, relaxed-looking wag usually means "I'm happy" or "let's play." However, a tail that is making short, rapid wags while held up very straight and stiff can mean "I'm the boss of this trail. Back off, or else."

This dog might be saying, "Don't come any closer. I'm warning you!"

Something else the two dog owners didn't know about was a recent experiment by Professor Giorgio Vallortigara, a scientist who specializes in animal behavior. Vallortigara observed thirty dogs over a period of twenty-five days. Ten times a day, for a minute each time, the dogs were shown their owners, another friendly human, a friendly cat, or a strange dog that was known to be a fighter. Every time the dogs saw one of the humans or the cat, their tails wagged mostly to the right side of their bodies. However, whenever the dogs saw the unfriendly dog, their tails wagged to the left. Professor Vallortigara concluded that a right-wag signals friendliness, while a left-wag signals fear or anger.

The story of Harold and Midnight is a good example of how accepting commonly held beliefs without questioning them can get people—and their pets—into trouble. The best way to understand any subject is to question what is believed to be true, rather than simply accept it.

When it comes to the subject of pets—the animals so many people think of as their best friends—knowing the facts about their behavior is essential. Good information helps us to understand our pets and take better care of them.

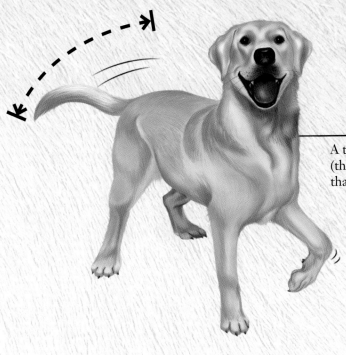

A tail wagging to the right (the viewer's left) signals that a dog feels friendly.

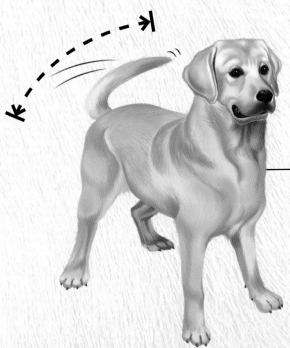

A tail wagging to the left (the viewer's right) signals that a dog feels upset.

One Life, Not Nine

A cat has exactly the same number of lives as every other living thing—one. The saying that they have nine comes from an old **superstition**. However, it's true that cats can perform feats that would hurt or kill many other animals.

For example, a cat can easily stroll along the tops of narrow fences or along high tree branches without falling. A cat walks like a tightrope walker, putting one foot directly in front of the other. It uses its tail the way a tightrope walker uses a pole for balance.

A cat can also jump down from high places, landing gracefully and safely on its feet—most of the time. Even if a cat falls, which sometimes does happen, it usually lands on its feet.

If and when a cat falls, its brain tells its body exactly what to do. Automatically, without thinking, the cat twists and turns in the air. Meanwhile, it spreads out its legs to slow the fall as a parachute would. Finally, the cat's back arches upward to absorb some of the shock of hitting the ground.

Even cats can get injured.

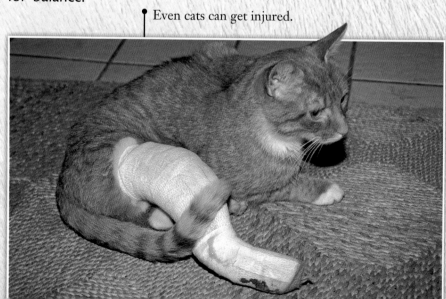

So yes—cats are tightrope walkers, gymnasts, and daredevils. But they have just one life. Even a cat can be hurt or killed by falling from a high window, to say nothing of being hit by a car or being attacked by another animal. Cats need to be cared for and kept safe, just as much as any other pet.

Without even thinking about it, a cat twists, turns, and spreads its body so that it usually ends up landing safely on its feet.

Cats Are *Not* Witches

The belief that a cat can die and come back to life nine times probably dates to the time when people believed in witchcraft. A book called *Beware the Cat*, published in England in 1584, warned that cats were witches in disguise, and that a witch could take on the body of her cat nine times.

Breathing Underwater

Fish, like all animals, need oxygen to live. They don't come up to the surface to breathe, and they don't swim around with snorkels or little scuba tanks. They get their oxygen from the water.

When a fish's mouth is open, it's taking in water. When a fish closes its mouth, it's taking oxygen out of the water with its **gills** before pumping the water back out of its body.

Unlike fish, humans need special equipment to breathe underwater.

Oxygen being used by fish needs to be replaced, and fresh oxygen may enter the water in several ways— from the air above the water and from underwater plants and tiny organisms that give off oxygen. This new oxygen dissolves, the way sugar dissolves if stirred into a glass of water.

Pet fish get oxygen in the same way as fish in nature do. Oxygen from the room enters the water, so a fish bowl or tank should never be tightly covered. Plants also add oxygen to the water. Plastic plants may look pretty in an aquarium, but they aren't much use to fish.

How a Fish Breathes

A fish breathes by opening its mouth and taking in water. The water flows over the fish's gills. Oxygen dissolved in the water passes from the gills into the fish's bloodstream and is circulated throughout its body.

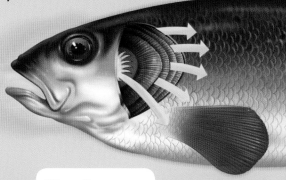

Water flows in through the mouth.

Water flows over the gills, then out.

Lovebirds in Love?

"Ever since Jenna and her boyfriend met, they've been just like a pair of lovebirds" is an example of how the term "lovebirds" is used to describe humans. A lovebird is actually a small, short-tailed African parrot.

Lovebirds get their name from the fact that their favorite pastime is sitting side by side with their mates. Also, pairs like to feed each other. When one bird transfers food from its mouth to its mate's mouth, the birds look as if they're kissing.

The question "Do they really love each other?" is part of some even bigger questions: Do animals feel the same emotions as humans? And also, what *do* we mean by "love"?

A growing number of **biologists** and animal behaviorists today believe that many animals do feel love and other emotions. For example, biologist Marc Bekoff believes that emotions in animals aren't so different from human emotions. Bekoff said that emotions "serve as a social glue to bond animals with one another...."

Lovebirds are popular pets because they're affectionate, playful, and fun to watch.

Many people assume that having only one lovebird as a pet is wrong because the bird will become lonely and depressed. In fact, it can be fun to have just one lovebird. The bird will bond with its owner, as it would with another bird. But bird owners who cannot spend much time with their pet should get two lovebirds to keep each other company.

Training a Hamster

Your pet hamster probably won't give you a "high five" or roll over on command. But hamsters can be trained to do more than most people think. In fact, many animals that no one would even consider trying to train can be taught to respond to humans. It's all done by a method called **conditioning**.

Here's how it works. Say you want to train your hamster to sit up on its hind legs when you say "Sit up!" Follow these steps:

1. Hold a hamster treat up above the hamster's head.
2. Say "Sit up!" Always use slow movements and a soft voice so the hamster won't be frightened.

Hamsters can be trained using a method called "conditioning."

3. Repeat the command "Sit up!" until the hamster sits up to get the treat. Repeat this a few times, not a lot. At first, training sessions of two minutes are long enough. (Note that animals like dogs have a different form of conditioning, and words are not repeated.)

4. After quite a few days, the hamster will associate that hand motion and the sound of the command with the treat.

5. After much practice and repetition, the hamster will sit up when you put your hand above its head and say "Sit up!" even if it doesn't get a treat every time.

The same basic technique should work to teach your hamster to do other "tricks" such as coming to you or running through a tunnel made from a paper towel tube. This method—conditioning—works in a similar way for many kinds of animals.

Conditioning Works

In an interview, animal trainer Gary Gero spoke about his experiences training animals for the movies. He says that conditioning works with dogs, cats, birds, and even alligators, zebras, and flies. Gary's company, Birds and Animals Unlimited, trained the animals for the film *Harry Potter and the Chamber of Secrets*. The company's motto is "Any animal you want!"

Cat and Mouse

Torture is cruel, and cats are not cruel—no more so than any animal that kills other animals for food. These animals, called **predators**, are just doing what comes naturally. In other words, they are acting on **instinct**.

Cats, especially, have a bad reputation for being mean or cruel because of the particular way they hunt and kill their **prey**. A cat spots a mouse or another small animal, creeps up on it silently, springs, and pounces. In the end, the cat will kill its victim by a swift bite to the back of the neck. But first, the cat will often swat its victim around.

This is not because the cat enjoys seeing its victim suffer. It's really for the cat's self-protection. If the prey is stunned or unconscious, it can't fight back or harm the cat when the cat moves in close enough to deliver the killing bite.

Another question about pet cats is why they hunt at all. After all, cat owners feed their cats food from the store. Their next meal is only a can-opener away, so why kill? The answer is that a house cat is not so different from its wild **ancestors**, the big cats—lions, tigers, leopards, and panthers. They are just natural-born hunters.

Indoor Cats

Many cat owners keep their cats indoors so they will not kill other animals, especially birds. Other cat owners think it's mean to deprive a cat of living in its natural way. The fact is that indoor cats can be perfectly happy if their owners play with them. A cat can use its hunting instincts by pouncing on toys and batting them around the room.

Homeward Bound

Stories about lost dogs that found their way home have always been popular. One example is the story of an Airedale named Max, who was in a car accident forty-five miles (seventy-two kilometers) from his home. The frightened dog ran into the woods. Three weeks later, his owner was delighted to find Max in his backyard. And then there's Jarvis, the Jack Russell terrier from Cornwall, England, who found his way home by taking a ferryboat!

Both these stories were documented in the news. Many scientists, however, doubt stories about dogs that found their way home over hundreds or thousands of miles. Some say the dogs wandered around and arrived home by accident. Some say the stories are made up.

Yet others have **theories** that dogs can find their way by detecting the earth's magnetic fields, tracking the position of the sun, or even using some mysterious sense that humans don't understand. None of these theories has been scientifically tested.

On the other hand, scientists know that dogs do have extremely keen senses of smell and hearing. Any familiar sound, such as lake water lapping on a shore, or smell, such as the scent left by the tires of a car, would help a dog find its way home.

Jarvis became famous when his story was reported in the news.

No matter what you believe, all pets should be kept safe at home. If they get lost, they might not be as lucky as Max or Jarvis!

Fish Without Eggs

Almost all fish lay eggs, but a small percent give birth to live young, or "**fry**," as baby fish are called. The guppy is one type of fish that gives birth to live young. It's fascinating to watch the fry being born, but here's a warning to owners of pet guppies. These fish can have so many babies that they fill up a tank. If owners do nothing and let nature take its course, most of the fry will be eaten by larger fish. People who want to raise guppies should keep the fry in a separate tank until they are big enough to survive with the larger guppies.

guppy

fry

A tiny fry has just been born. The dark, puffy part of the female guppy's body contains more fry. The dark spot is the eyes of the fry about to be born.

The male cardinal fish protects its eggs by keeping them in its mouth. The male doesn't eat until the fry have hatched.

Fish that do lay eggs often scatter them around plants or onto gravel. Some lay eggs that stick to plants, rocks, or the glass sides of an aquarium. Most of the eggs will meet the same fate as the baby guppies. They will become fish food.

Most fish do not protect their eggs or their babies at all, but there are some exceptions. Bettas and gouramis lay their eggs in a nest of bubbles blown by the male fish. The male guards the bubble nest until the fry have hatched. Some male fish, such as cardinal fish and certain catfish, protect their eggs by keeping them in their mouths. They don't eat at all until their babies are hatched, and even then they don't go after the fry. And the male seahorse keeps the eggs in a pouch that's a bit like a kangaroo's.

eggs

Night Vision?

No animal—not even a cat—can see in total darkness. All animals need at least a little bit of light in order to see. However, cats' reputation for being able to see in the dark is not entirely undeserved. It is true that, in very dim light, cats can detect movements and shapes that would be invisible to humans.

Cats are able to see in semidarkness because their eyes make better use of light than the eyes of many other animals. Deep inside a cat's eye is a layer of glittering cells that acts like a mirror. It reflects light onto the **retina**— the light-sensitive structure in the eye that makes vision possible. The glow in cats' eyes is called "eyeshine."

The "mirror" in a cat's eye increases the amount of light shining on the retina, making it easier for cats to see in very dim light. It also makes their vision slightly blurry in very bright light. For these reasons, the best time for cats to see clearly—and the best time for them to hunt—is just after dawn and just before dark.

Although cats can't see on a pitch-dark night, they can still get around pretty well, relying on their keen senses of smell and hearing. They also use their whiskers, which are so sensitive to touch that they keep cats from running into objects when it's too dark for them to see.

The same structure in cats' eyes that lets them see in dim light makes their eyes seem to glow. This glow is called "eyeshine."

Animals with Eyeshine

Eyeshine can also be seen in the eyes of owls, foxes, and other animals that are active at night.

Talking with Dogs

"Come!" "Sit!" "Stay!" Most dogs can learn to obey these few simple commands. When a dog hears the word "sit," it sits, and it receives a treat and a pat. In the future, the dog associates sitting on command with getting a treat and an expression of love from its owner.

It's simple to teach a dog a few commands, but some dogs have a surprisingly large human-language vocabulary. For example, a border collie named Rico, tested by scientists in Germany, showed that he knew the names for more than 200 toys. Rico can go to a pile of toys and pick up the one his owner asks for by name.

In a similar test, another dog named Chaser has shown that she knows the names for more than 1,000 toys. Chaser has a larger vocabulary than most three-year-old children!

However, **linguists**— scientists who study language—say that there is more to language than associating sounds with objects. For example, a dog might know the word "pencil," but it won't know that the pencil is used for writing, that it's different from a pen, and so on. Also, dogs can't understand words for ideas such as "happiness," "freedom," or "beauty." And they don't get jokes!

Chaser sits with the hundreds of toys that she knows the names of.

Still, dog owners enjoy having "conversations" with their dogs, and there's no reason for them to stop. The dogs like the attention, and talking to a pet makes people feel good.

"Parroting" Language

Many parrots can squawk out "hello" or "pretty birdy," but that isn't exactly talking. The birds are just "parroting," or imitating sounds without knowing what they mean. However, three parrots have recently made people take what parrots say more seriously.

Cosmo is an African gray parrot whose owner, Betty Jean Craige, is a college professor. Craige reports that when she leaves for work, Cosmo says, "Betty Jean be back soon, okay?" Craige has written a book called *Conversations with Cosmo*.

Arielle—another noted conversationalist—is Mike Dalton's blue and gold **macaw**. Arielle can say around 3,000 words and phrases and often seems to know what she's talking about. For example, Dalton taught Arielle the word "water." Later, crossing a puddle on a sidewalk, Arielle said the word "wet." Dalton said, "That blew me away. If the bird can transfer meanings to new situations, we now have communication."

Irene Pepperberg with Alex, an African gray parrot

Alex was an African gray owned by a well-known animal behaviorist named Irene Pepperberg. In her book *Alex and Me*, Pepperberg describes how she taught Alex to say many words and sentences and to identify fifty objects, seven colors and shapes, and quantities of up to six.

Pepperberg does not call Alex's speech "language." In an interview she said, "Language is what you and I are doing, an incredibly complex form of communication." Still, Cosmo, Arielle, and Alex have shown the world that parrots are more than just ordinary birdbrains.

In Living Color

Many people believe that dogs can't see colors, but they can. The colors they see just aren't as bright as the colors humans see. Dogs don't see the world in very sharp detail, either. But don't feel sorry for dogs. Colors and details don't matter so much to them.

What really does matter to a dog is the one thing a dog's eyes are especially good at seeing—motion. Dogs can see something move the tiniest bit, even if it is far away. This sensitivity to the slightest motion is important to any hunting animal. The hunter can spot moving prey far in the distance and follow it, even if it runs fast and far.

Of course, pet dogs don't

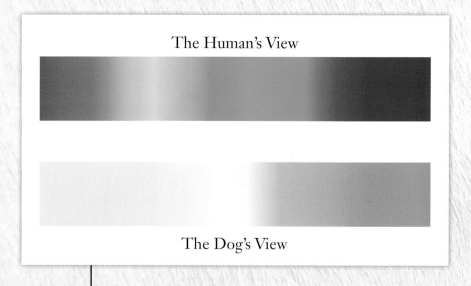

The Human's View

The Dog's View

Humans can see more colors than dogs. Tests show that dogs can't tell the difference between red, yellow, orange, or green, but they can see whites, light blues, purples, and different shades of gray.

Humans would see the rabbit as it is shown in the photo on the left. The photo on the right shows how a dog would see the same scene.

have to chase down their food. They get their food from humans. But dogs are the descendants of wild animals—wolves. They have inherited the urge to hunt and the skills to be good at it.

Hunting instincts explain why so many dogs like to chase anything that moves—a ball, a stick, a cat, or even a car or bicycle. Dog owners should keep this in mind. Anyone who has a dog with an irresistible urge to chase should make sure the dog stays on a leash or under supervision. That way the dog stays safe, and so does the neighbor's cat!

Homing Instinct

Pigeons can find their way home over hundreds or even thousands of miles. And they have been doing it for thousands of years.

Three thousand years ago, the Egyptians used pigeons to deliver messages attached to the birds' legs. And, in 776 B.C.E., pigeons carried messages from Greece to other countries announcing the winners of the Olympic Games. In fact, "pigeon post" was the fastest communication system until Samuel Morse invented the telegraph in 1844. Even after that, pigeons carried important messages to soldiers in both World War I and World War II. One pigeon trained by the United States Army flew 2,300 miles (3,701 kilometers) to reach its destination!

Today, people enter pet pigeons in races all over the world. The birds are driven away from their homes and are released at the same time. The first one to make it home is the winner—and just about all of them make it home.

There's no doubt that pigeons have the ability to find their homes over long distances, but scientists don't know yet how they do it. Perhaps they use the position of the sun. Maybe they can sense the magnetic field that surrounds Earth. It's possible that they use their sense of smell. Scientists keep experimenting with pigeons, but the mystery has not been solved yet.

Your Turn

Maybe some of the facts in this book surprised you. Maybe not. Either way, if you want to get it right about pets or any topic, don't just accept what seems to be true or what people say. Instead, take two steps.

Step One: Ask questions.

Step Two: Do research. Find out what the experts have to say.

If you have pets, it's important to understand their needs and behavior. But even if you don't own any animals, they're part of the natural world. Asking questions and doing your research will always help you understand more about the world you live in.

Glossary

ancestors (AN-ses-tuhrs) n., family members who lived a long time ago

behaviorists (bi-HEY-vyuhr-ists) n., scientists who study behavior

biologists (bahy-AH-luh-jists) n., scientists who study biology, the science of living things

conditioning (kuhn-DIH-shu-ning) n., using rewards for the repeated performance of a particular action

fry (FRAHY) n., baby fish

gills (GILS) n., organs used for getting oxygen from the water

instinct (IN-stingt) n., behavior that is natural, rather than learned

linguists (LING-gwists) n., scientists who study language

macaw (muh-KOH) n., a kind of parrot

predators (PRE-duh-tuhrs) n., animals that hunt and kill other animals for food

prey (PREY) n., animals that are hunted and eaten by other animals

retina (RUH-tuh-nuh) n., the lining at the back of the eyeball. The retina is sensitive to light and sends images to the brain.

superstition (soo-puhr-STIH-shun) n., a belief based on magic rather than science or fact

theories (THEE-uh-rees) n., ideas that explain how or why something happens

Index

breathing 8–9

bubble nests 19

cats 6–7, 14–15, 20–21

color 26–27

conditioning 12–13

dog's tail 2–5

dogs 2–5, 16–17, 22–23, 26–27

eggs (fish) 18–19

eyes 20–21

eyeshine 21

fighting 3

fish 8–9, 18–19

Gero, Gary 13

guppies 18–19

hamsters 12–13

hunting 14–15

instinct 14–15, 27–29

killing 14–15

language 22–23, 24–25

love 10–11

lovebirds 10–11

parrots 24–25

pigeons 28–29

plants 9

superstition 6

training 12–13

vision 20–21, 26–27

water 8–9

whiskers (cat's) 21

witchcraft 7